THE SILLY SPY JOKEBOOK

St. Brigid School
730 Citadel Way NW
Calgary, Alberta

by Chris Tait

Kidsbooks
Incorporated

Copyright © 2002 Kidsbooks, Inc.
230 Fifth Avenue
New York, NY 10001

Manufactured in Canada

Visit us at www.kidsbooks.com

What do you call an underwater secret agent?

James Pond!

Why was Quasimodo such a good secret agent?

Because he always had a hunch!

Where do spies go when they die?

To double-oh-heaven!

What do you call a secret agent with great vision?

An eye spy!

Why did the spy spend the day
in bed?
> Because he was told
> to stay undercover!

What kind of shoes do athletic
spies wear?
> Sneak-ers!

What game do young spies learn on
the playground?
> Hide-and-seek!

What is a secret agent's favorite
car game?
> I Spy!

What is a spy's favorite dessert?
S-pie!

What do you call a secret agent who spies for both sides?
Double trouble!

Why should you never play hide-and-seek with spies?
Because they always sneak a peek!

Why did the spy think something was wrong?
Because she had a sneaking suspicion!

How do you pass a test in spy school?
You cheat without getting caught!

What kind of food do
super-sleuths love?
Spy-see food!

What does the Secret Service call
its yellow-haired spy?
James Blonde!

Why was the spy so afraid
of insects?
Because he knew that he
was being bugged!

What did the spy say when she found out that her phone was tapped?

"When will these guys stop bugging me?"

What did the detective say to the chicken?

"I have to appre-hen-d you!"

What kind of critters do secret agents like?

Spy-ders!

Why did the spy think that the floor had lips?

Because she knew that the walls had ears!

What do spies give each other when they get married?

Decoder rings!

What did the American spy say when he had the proof?

C I A-in't lying!

Why did the spy handbook seem
so empty?

**Because it was written in
invisible ink!**

Who is a secret agent's favorite
superhero?

Spy-derman!

What did the undercover agent name
his dog?

Snoop-y!

What did the supervillain say to
the spy?

"It ain't easy being mean!"

Who did the secret agent's reckless driver work for?

The Secret Swerve-ice!

Why did the spy say, "Keep your ear to the ground?"

Because he was listening for his shoe phone!

What villain is the most disagreeable?

Dr. No!

What do you call a spy who's a bug?

Insect-or Gadget!

What do spies use to open
secret doors?

A snea-key!

What did the spy discover about the
laundered money?

It was a cover-up!

What is a young spy's favorite
TV show?

Blue's Clues!

What did the detective say to the
handy spy?

"You're crafty!"

Why did the spy dig a hole in her backyard?

To hide her trenchcoat!

What do you call two spies in a diner?

Counter—espionage!

What does an undercover optometrist sell?

Spy glasses!

What do you call a wire-tapping rabbit spy?

Bugs bunny!

What do you call a spy who specializes in spying on houses?

A real estate agent!

What do you call someone who spies overseas?

A travel agent!

What do you call twin spies?

Double agents!

What do you call a villain who tells on other villains?
Gold Finker!

What was the code name of the spy sent to the North Pole?
Cold Finger!

What do you call the secret records of forestry spies?
The Ax Files!

What do you call a secret agent who just came back from Fort Knox?
The spy who came in from the gold!

How do spies make themselves look twice as good?

With bi-noculars!

What did the secret agent use to break out of her cell?

An X-file!

What kind of car do secret agents drive?

A spy-lark!

How do decoding agents like their eggs?

Un-scrambled!

Why did the retired spy think he could be a blacksmith?
Because he knew how to forge things!

What did the spy use when he didn't know the answer on a test?
Guess-pionage!

Where do spies go when they die?
Underground!

Why did the spy hide in the bushes?
Because she wanted to
hedge her bets!

Why did the spy think that he
could dance?
Because he knew how
to wire tap!

What does a spy wear under
his pants?
Stealth bloomers!

Where does a spy keep her leftovers?

Under wraps!

What do secret agents drink their juice out of?

Spy glasses, of course!

How does a spy finish his book in the dark?

With infra-read glasses!

Why didn't the spy take any pictures while on vacation?

Because he had a hidden camera!

What did the secret agent call her stolen torch?

A flashloot!

Where do secret agents live?

If I told you, it wouldn't be a secret!

What do spies call a bad day of catching fish?

Fishin' Impossible!

What do spies say to each other
when they make a toast?
"Here's to your stealth!"

How do secret agents look
for fingerprints?
With magni-spying glasses!

What do colorful secret
agents wear?
Spy-dye!

What do canine spies practice?
Cloak and dogger!

What do spies call it when they take off their underwear?

De-briefing!

What do spies do when they have a slow day?

Mission wishin'!

How do spy magicians start their tricks?

By saying, "Pick a lock, any lock!"

How do computer spies know that it's time to go to work?

They have a big hack attack!

Why did the computer spy quit
his job?
> **Because he just couldn't
> hack the pressure!**

What do you call a dim-witted spy?
> **Counter-intelligent!**

What did the secret agent have
for lunch?
> **A spy sub!**

What do you call a rural spy?
> **An in-farmer!**

What did the spy say when she was questioned?

"I swear it's the sleuth!"

What do spy kids do for fun?

They go to Scout meetings!

What do you call a ghost spy?

A spook!

What did the spy dog say about sneaking around?

"It's a ruff job, but somebody's got to do it!"

Why did the spy keep checking his timepiece?

> **Because he was told to keep watch for the enemy!**

What do you call a spy who is always out of breath?

> **The Pink Pant-er!**

What did the spy call the difficult task he was given?

> **Mission improbable!**

Why was the bounty hunter looking for a man with a tag in his hair?
Because he heard that there was a price on his head!

What do you call the canine unit of the Secret Service?
The Federal Beagle of Investigation!

How did the American spy find his foreign friend?
He did a background Czech!

How did the spy feel when she tripped a wire at the embassy?
Alarmed!

Where do spies plant their
secret gardens?

Behind investi-gates!

What did they say about the
successful spy?

He had a great track record!

What should every sloppy
spy have?

A license to spill!

What do you call a great spy?

A super snooper!

What do you call a snoop with sticky feet?

A gumshoe!

What do you call a detective with an eye patch?

A pirate investigator!

What do you call a sleuth with a big bill?

Private Duck!

What did the spy say when he was caught by the government?

"Gee, man!" (G-man)

Why do cats make good spies?
Because they know how to prowl!

Why do gophers make good spies?
**Because they know how
to dig for dirt!**

Why do ghosts make good detectives?
**Because they're not afraid to
find skeletons in the closet!**

What do you call a tall spy?
Lurk!

What did the spy say after she processed her film?
"This is an interesting development!"

Why do farmers make good secret agents?
Because they don't mind raking a little muck!

Why did the spy have to be quiet in the cornfield?
Because there were ears everywhere!

Why did the spy hate potatoes?
Because all the eyes made
him nervous!

What did the sick spy say about her
code name?
"I don't like this ail-ias!"

What did the secret agent say when
he saw that it was raining?
"Make sure you put on
your rain code!"

What did the secret agent do when
he got on board the boat?
He performed a ship-search!

Why was the left-handed spy so afraid of being arrested?

Because she didn't want to be read her rights!

What do you call a royal who has been arrested for spying?

A finger prince!

What does a spy use to look for clues on a lawn?

Magnifying grass!

How did the unhappy spy feel when he had no leads?

He had the no-clues blues!

Why did the spy dog like to be taken for a walk?

Because it knew that it would have a good lead!

What do you call a spying royal with a shoe phone?

Foot prince!

Why is it hard to get a date when you're a spy?

Because everyone thinks you're creepy!

What advice do you give to a spy
who can't open a window?
"If at first you don't succeed,
pry, pry again!"

What do you call a spy who is slow
to look for clues?
A slowpoke!

What do spies wear to
fancy dinners?
In-former attire!

What do you call a story about a
spy who spills the beans?
A tattletale!

What kind of bird always talks under pressure?

A stool pigeon!

What is an old spy's favorite song?

"Jimmy Crack Code"!

What goes dot–dot–dash–dash–squeak?

Mouse code!

How did the spy get tossed out
of school?
They gave him a
sneaking suspension!

What do you call an accused spy
with his finger in his nose?
A sus-picked!

What do you call a group of spies?
The hunch bunch!

Why was the spy nicknamed
"The Cobra"?
Because he always had a
snaking suspicion!

What made the sleuth so theatrical?
She was always at the
scene of the crime!

Why did the secret agent think that
his dog was a spy?
Because he caught it
sniffing around!

Why did the spy put banana peels on
his shoes?
So he could slip behind
enemy lines!

Why did the sleuth think that something was up when he got to the seafood store?

Because he smelled something fishy!

Why was the spy unhappy to have a nickel?

Because she wanted to have a sixth cent!

Why did the secret agent think that spy school would be so expensive?

She just had an in-tuition!

What was the slogan of the Nordic
spy who lived at the North Pole?
"Snow problem!"

How did the spy learn to see in
the dark?
He went to night-vision school!

Who did the spies report to
when they saw someone creeping
in the woods?
Their branch manager!

Why did the spy hate writing
reports on his computer?
Because he just wasn't that type!

What did the skating spy say when he fell and dropped his computer files on the ice?

"I've got a slipped disk!"

What made the robot secret agent act crazy?

He had a couple of screws loose!

Why did the scuba-diving agent feel so low?

Because she had a sinking feeling!

What happened to the scuba spy?
He tanked!

Why didn't the spy want to dive to the sunken sub?

He couldn't handle the pressure!

What did the spy kitten want to be when it grew up?

A cat burglar!

What did the spy say to his friend who was hiding behind the curtain?

"Pull yourself together!"

What did the secret agent say to the camping spy?

"You're so tents!"

Why did the spy hate to play cards at the casino?
Because she found them hard to deal with!

Why did the scuba spy hate it when his phone rang underwater?
Because it left a wringing in his ears!

Why did the detective think that snooping around an apple farm would help him solve the case?

He thought he would get to the core of it!

Why didn't the spy want to look for clues in the trash?

Because he thought it was a waste of time!

What did the spy say after she got poison ivy from spying in the bushes?

"I made a rash decision!"

What did the spy think about having to drill peepholes in a wall all day?

That it was really boring!

Where did the feline spy keep
its gear?

In the tool cat!

Why did the spy think the forgery
ring was hilarious?

Because of all the funny money!

What did the spy think after he was
bitten by mosquitoes in the swamp?

That he was a sucker for
taking the job!

Why did the spy put a banana peel
in front of his closet?

So he could slip into something
more comfortable!

Why did the spy go to work dressed as a bee?

> **Because she heard that there was going to be a sting!**

Why did the spy nickname his enemy "The Spider"?

> **Because he lived in a web of lies!**

What did the martial-arts spy drink in the afternoon?

> **Kara-tea!**

What did the spy say about his enemy who got out of the cheese factory?

> **"He made a grate escape!"**

Why wasn't the spy surprised that his enemy wanted to lower him into boiling oil?

Because it was Fry-day!

What did the spy have to take after being bitten by a bug?
Ant-ibiotics!

What did the spy say to the bee?
"Buzz off!"

How did the spy feel when the enemy agent stole his shoes?
De-feeted!

What did the spy say when someone asked, "Did I just see you snooping?"

"Gee, I hope not!"

Why did the spy wear two pairs of glasses?

Because he wanted to have four-sight!

What do you call a spy movie set at the North Pole?

A chiller thriller!

What did the perfumed agent say to the spy?

"Did you get the secret message I scent?"

What did the spy hear on his shoe phone when he was put on hold?

Sole music!

Why was the sleuth spending so much time around the chicken coop?

Because she suspected fowl play!

What did she say when she found out that she was right?

"Eggs-actly as I thought!"

How did the cowboy spy communicate with the home office?

By saddle-lite!

What did Sherlock Holmes say to his friend about grade school for spies?

"It's elementary, my dear Watson!"

What do you call a spy with a runny nose?

A dribble agent!

What did the man say when he uncovered the slouching spy?

"Im-posture!"

What did the spy call the comedian double agent?

A funny phony!

What did the secret agent think about the time he spent spying on a rabbit farm?

That it was a hare-raising adventure!

Why do international spies always want to run the world?

Because they love jog-raphy!

What did the secret agent say when she heard about the giant spy?
"This sounds like a tall tale to me!"

How can you check to see if your friends are enemy agents?
With a spy-detector test!

Where did the secret agent find the sketch artist?
In the drawing room, of course!

Why don't piano spies ever catch an enemy?
Because they just can't get organ-ized!

Why did the hacker give his
computer a box of tissues?
Because it had a nasty virus!

What did the secret agent say when
he caught his enemy hiding under
his bed?
"You're under a-rest!"

What did the secret agent say
when he found his enemy hiding in
his closet?
"You're under a-vest!"

What did the French spy say after
hiding out in the rain all night?
"Eiffel a cold coming on!"

What did the secret agent say when he finally captured his enemy, the Condor?

"Now you're a jailbird!"

What did the spy say when he was told to make a peephole in the wall?

"Yeah, I know the drill!"

Why did the peace-loving spy hate fiddles?

Because he didn't believe in violins! (violence)

What did the secret agent think about chasing her nemesis through the train?

That he was hard to keep track of!

What did the spy student think when he broke his pencil?

He thought it was pointless!

What do deep—sea spies have for lunch?

Subs!

What did the rock—climbing spy wear for jewelry?

Mountain-earrings!

What did the spy say when he couldn't find clues in the forest?
"I'm stumped!"

What did the enemy spy say when he couldn't find clues in the aluminum factory?
"Curses, foiled again!"

What happened to the agent-in-training who flunked spelling in spy school?
He was ex-spelled!

What did the sketch artist say
about his job to the secret agent?
"It has some draw-backs!"

What did the computer spy say when
she found the enemy's plans?
"This is disk-usting!"

Where was the scuba spy afraid
to swim?
In the Dead Sea!

What did the spy say when he tied
up his enemy in record time?
"Knot so fast!"

Why didn't the spy want to kiss
the frog?

**Because she was afraid it
would croak!**

What do secret agents use to look
for their enemies?

Spy-noculars!

What did the sleuth say after he'd
been out looking for clues all night?

"Owl never do that again!"

What did the spy say when she got
a splinter in her hand?

"Wooden you know it!"

How long did the spy stay under-cover in the treehouse?

About a fort-night!

How do spies feel after laying low all the time?

A little flat!

How did the spy feel after spending a month in Turkey?

Stuffed!

What did the spy say when he heard that there was an invisibility pill?

"I find that hard to swallow!"

What do spies wear when they are in the desert?

Camel-flage!

How did the spy feel after hiding in a mine all day?

A little coaled!

What did the spy do when he heard that he had to dig a tunnel?

He tried to worm his way out of it!

What do you call it when a spy almost gets shot by a crossbow user?

An arrow escape!

What did the secret agent think about spying at the zoo?

That it was aardvark!
(hard work)

Why was the female spy behind enemy lines?

Because it was a no-man's land!

What did the spy think about her job on the moon?

She thought that it lacked atmosphere!

What did the sick spy think of his doctor when she told him that he was just ducky?

He thought the doctor was a quack!

What did the spy say when he had to row himself back to shore?
"This is oar-ibble!"

What did the secret agent say to the space-age spy?
"Pleased to meteor!"

What did the silly agent say when his friend asked him to call him a cab?
"Ok, you're a cab!"

What made the spy think that he had evidence against the lint?
Because he had it all on tape!

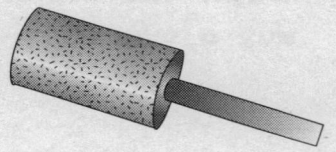

What did they call the double agent who was always calling home?
A phone-y!

What do you call a spy who ends up in jail?
Con-fidential!

Why was the spy looking in the want ads?
Because the information she needed was classified!

What did the spy say when he left his papers in his filing cabinet?

"I'll have to check with the bureau on that one!"

What did the spy say when he split his pants?

"Let me check my briefs!"

What did the secret agent say when he tracked down the lost goalie?

"Finders keepers!"

What did the secret agent say when she was looking for the missing livestock?

"Ollie, ollie, oxen free!"

What did the secret agent say when he mistook a bison for a cow?

"Sorry, it was an ox-idant!"

What do spies put at the top of every memo?

Re: search!

What did the computer spy get from the Internet virus?

A hacking cough!

What did the spy say when his canine companion defected?

"Doggone it!"

Where did the detective find the missing porridge?

In the mush room!

What did the spy say when he woke to find two Xs written on him?

"I've been double-crossed!"

What do you call a spy with bad posture?

A stooped snoop!

What do you call testimony that doesn't stand up in court?

Wilt-ness!

What do you ask a secret agent to do in court?

Testi-spy!

What do you pay a secret agent to speak in court?

Testi-money!

What did the secret agent call the bowling ball that he took to court?

Heavy-dence!

What do Viking spies use to communicate?

Norse code!

Why did the spy know to look for the enemy agent in the wild?
Because he was a cheat-ah!

What did the sign on the nuclear lab door say when the spy arrived?
Gone fission!

Where did the spy have to go to find the enemy spy's baker?
To his secret breadquarters!

Where did the secret agent find the enemy chef?

In her hidden fork-tress!

What did the spy wearing shorts say to the secret agent?

Meet me at the cut-offs!

How did the spy know that his enemy would come out of his underground lair?

Because he always caved in!

How did the heavy spy escape?

He dug a ton-el!

What did the detective say when he caught the cold-hearted killer?
"Freeze!"

What did the spy say when she caught someone snooping in her front yard?
"Stop in the name of the lawn!"

What code name did they give to the spy who chewed gum?
Bubble-oh-seven!

Why did the secret agent look for clues in a pasture?
Because he wanted to do his first field assignment!

Why do spies love the snow?
Because it's a hint-er wonderland!

What did the detective say to the dessert?
"I have to put you in protective custard-y!"

Why did Soviet spies always wear mittens?
Because they were in the Cold War!

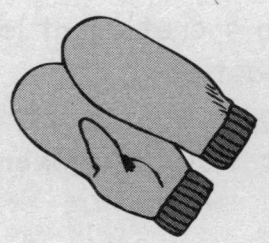

What did the silly sleuth say to
the conductor?
"I have to de-train you
for questioning!"

What did the secret agent with the
cold say to the criminal?
"Hold out your hands so
I can cough you!"

Why did the spy follow her enemy
to the races?
Because she wanted
to track him down!

What happened to the sketch artist?
He disappeared without a trace!

What did the secret agent say to
the Riddler?

I have to take you in
for questioning!

Why was the spy hiding in the
butcher shop?

Because she thought it was
where the steak-out was!

What do secret agents do for fun?
Play catch!

What do you call it when a secret
agent comes out of hiding?
Dis-cover!

Why was the spy worried about his socks while spying on the golfers?
Because he had a hole in one!

Why was the spy afraid of planes?
Because she was afraid that someone would identi-fly her!

What did the secret agent use to write his autobiography?
Sus-pens!

Why did the spy's horse retire?
Because its nerves were shod!

How did the spy feel when he put his hand on the spark plug?
A little shocked!

Where did the secret agent catch the dirty crook?
At the scene of the grime!

What do countries call it when they trade agents?
Spy for a spy!

When do villains get read their rights?
When they're in the wrong!

What did the secret agent say when he caught the slow spy?
"I've uncovered a vicious plod!"

How did the enemy secret agent like his food?
Scheming hot!

What do spies call the room where all their long meetings are held?
The bored room!

What did the spy find on the ship?
A conspira-sea!

What did the secret agent think of
the magician spy?
He was tricky!

What did the spy's cat think when
it saw the crime scene?
"I smell a rat!"

What do spies call their best
basketball squad?
The scheme team!

What did the secret agent say
about the suspicious chicken farmer?
**"I'll bet he's hatching a plan
right now!"**

What did the spy do while he
made dinner?
Cooked up a plot!

Why are spies so good at
playing softball?
Because they're underhanded!

What do you call a female spy?
Miss Chevious!

What do evil agents call their spy classes?

Wick Ed.!

Why was the detective suspicious of the Leaning Tower of Pisa?

Because there was something crooked about it!

What did the spy say about the phone conversation she was tapping?
"This is dial-bolical!"

What did the secret agent call the fishy spy?
A rap-scallion!

Why did the enemy's plan make the spy feel sad?
Because it was a blue print!

Where did the spy keep his fake beards hidden?
In his must-stash!

What did the gumshoe think of the spy?

That he was a heel!

Why did the spy hate being underground?

Because everyone else thought he was a lowlife!

What did the enemy spy call his speech about knots?

His tie-rant!

What do mean spies drink?

Nas-tea!

Why did the spy want a
green thumb?

**So he could plant things
on people!**

How did the spy get her broken-
down stealthmobile home?

She got a tip-tow!

Why didn't the secret agent like
the robot spy?

He just couldn't rust him!

Why did the detective think the
spy had wings?

Because he was a fly-by-night!

Why did the secret agent think the detective was a fake?
Because he was so un-real-iable!

What is another name for spy glasses?
Skeptical spectacles!

What do spies call hiding out at night?
Eve-ation! (evasion)

What did the detective say about the double agent climbing the wall?
"I hope he false down on the job!"

What did the spy call his new
hat disguise?

His false hood!

Why did the computer spy quit?

**Because he just couldn't
hack it anymore!**

What did the spy call the secret
hideout in the woods?

A real mis-tree!

What did the secret agent say
about the lying spy?

"He has bad moral fibber!"

What did the spy say about the sneaky bear?

"He's so fur-tive!"

What do you call a spy with many different disguises?

Two-faced!

What did the spies call the hidden passage that made the rug stick up?

The trip door!

What did the spies call their female boss?

Miss Chief!

What did the spy call the
fishy dealer?

A card shark!

How did the spy get to the honey?
She followed the path
of bee-trail! (betrayal)

Why didn't the spy trust the whale?
He knew it was a blubbermouth!

Why didn't the spy trust the car salesman?

> **Because she knew that he was a trader!**

What happened when the spy got caught on the enemy boat?

> **She was sent up the river!**

What did the secret agents call the spy who was dim-witted in court?

> **The evi-dunce!**

What do you call a spy who leaves dinner early?

> **A dessert-er!**

Why did the spy call the pat of
butter cowardly?

     Because it was yellow!

What did the spy call his
mother's sister?

     The auntie hero!

Why didn't anybody believe the
scuba spy?

     **Because he had no ground
to stand on!**

What do spies say to their children
when they are naughty?

     "You are under-grounded!"

What did the detective say when someone tried to hand him a phone?
"Just the fax, ma'am!"

What did the spy say when he couldn't find his magician son?
"I loose son!" (illusion)

What did the secret agent say about the spy who could pick pockets?
"He's slight of hand!"

Why did the ghost spy love his job?
Because he just couldn't phantom doing anything else!

What happened between the two opposing agents at the butchershop?
It was ham-to-ham combat!

Why was the spy afraid of the phone?
It was just one of her hang-ups!

How could the spy hear secrets in the swimming pool?
He knew how to read laps!

Why did the spy have to take
a sick day?

> Because she had
> strained her ears!

Why did the spy have a cast
on his ear?

> Because he had heard
> a broken code!

How did the spy see through the
suspect's poncho disguise?

> He just knew it was a put-on!

Why do detectives need glasses?

> Because they get hint squint!

How can spy submarines see so well?
**Because they're made
for deep-sea vision!**

What did Shakespeare call
his spy play?
A View to a Quill!

What happened to the spy with
bad vision?
He got a sight-ation! (citation)

What did the spy say when asked
how he missed seeing the suspect?
"Eye don't know!"

Why was the sniffing spy dog so full of duty?

Because it knew what it had been scent to do!

What did scientists try to develop in the lab to help spies?

Smell-o-vision!

What did the detective say to the spy dog?

"Would you stop hounding me!"

Where do spies rest in the middle of a long pursuit?

In their chase loungers!

Why were the spies so quiet while they laid their trap?

    Because they were waiting with baited breath!

What did the spy say about fishing for clues?

    "You really have to lure your standards!"

How did the detective catch his enemy at the pig farm?

    It was a ham-bush!

What do baby spies play with?

    Ploy toys!

What did the detective think about
the dancing lumberjack case?

It was a real jig-saw puzzle!

What happened when the spy's
dog lost the scent?

It got into a real furry flurry!

What do spies call members of
their club?

Their peers!

How did the spy know that he was
tired from spying all day?

**Because he just couldn't
get up the stares!**

Why do mummies make good spies?
Because they are good at keeping things under wraps!

What do you call it when one cow spies on another?
A steak-out!

How do spies send secret messages in the forest?
By moss code!

What happened when the spy slept
under the car?
She woke up oily the next morning!

What is a silly secret agent's
favorite movie?
Spy Hard!

What is a junior secret agent's
favorite movie?
Spy Kids, of course!

Where do sick spies go?
The ho-spy-tal!

Why did the secret agent cross
the road?
To catch the other spy!

How did the spy feel when he spilled
fruit punch on himself?
Like he was caught red-handed!

What did the secret agent give the
suspicious double-crossing spy?
A lie-defector test!

What is a spy's favorite TV show?
Hidden Camera!

What do double-crossing spies do on vacation?

They just lie around!

Why do informers smell so bad?
Because they're always spilling the beans!

What did the spy say when she found out that the king's son was missing?
"We'll have to dust for prince!"